Rusty Skies and Golden Winds

SANNIDHYA SHARMA

BlueRose ONE .com
Stories Matter

First Published in April 2022

ISBN: 978-93-5611-534-7

BLUEROSE PUBLISHERS

www.bluerosepublishers.com

info@bluerosepublishers.com

+91 8882 898 898

Cover Design:

Muskan Sachdeva

Typographic Design:

Ilma

Distributed by: BlueRose, Amazon, Flipkart

A Note From The Author

It is easy to look over what's not tempted by our souls, then again, who knows how many desires these seemingly useless things might help us fulfill, this book's creation didn't begin with bright ideas or lucky flukes, but by simply picking up things as worthless as a dead leaf and searching for all it hides. What may seem to simply be the last memory of yet another entity whose death is irrelevant can be mingled and mangled inside out and lo, the ends still meet. When you try to really be creative, as long as you have your hand to guide you, you will always be able to bring beauty to anything and everything. What I believe is that nature is most uncertain and certain at the same time, all we can do as mere mortals is to observe and understand what these fragile senses of ours feel. Its like randomly splattering colors on a canvas and letting the way in which the colors mix to choose what emerges on it. From how I look at it, we don't control our creativity, instead, it's the other way around, I look at us people as vehicles driven by faith and desire, creativity being what those two are called together because to fulfill our desires, we may try to shorten our ways and make quick work of all bottlenecks, we have belief, we have faith that our guesses born of confusion could help us win all we can. A gamble with nothing to lose is how I define creativity. This book "Rusty Skies and golden winds" may question common beliefs and norms. You may also find this relatable as it refers strongly to nature and the human mind, it may even help you to, as I call it "enhance" your perspective of this world. Overall, this book written by me is a simple request letter to everyone to think twice before they do.

Foreword

You are being schooled to sit yourself in a square. Just like the numbers you write on a math notebook. But you do not get better at it with practice. A child, you are destined to discover that the shape you're put into, needs a warping that only your arms can do. You keep from stretching them until you no longer can. And then as you mould the outlines of your existence, and as space is rendered amoebic, questions begin to hit you – fierce, rock solid drops of rain that hurt yet lead you to inescapable clarity.

Sannidhya is a young poet-philosopher with a rare insight and a strong character, who has embraced questions as a way of life. He lets them define the nature of the world in the moment. He lets himself be carried away by the unknown force and eyes the blood on the paper bravely.

Replete with metaphors, irony and word play, Sannidhya's verses boast of an inimitable originality. His brilliance, as he writes of life as simply as in the lines: Perching on a bench / Life's warming trace or in We strive to be broken / And let go of life / We hope to be frozen / And still stay alive, will not be lost on anyone who dares to read, write or philosophise.

His searing questions exude exemplary courage: Should one step forward / Into the dark? / Or should one strengthen / The enlightened part?

Sannidhya's is a young voice that befriends cacti as it does roses. As he attempts to solve, resolve and absolve, let us lend an ear to the songs he hears.

- Geetika Kohli Amla

Acknowledgments

I would like to express my gratitude towards my mentor, Mrs.Geetika Kohli Amla for her contribution and cooperation in the making of this book. I would like to extend my gratitude further to my parents for providing me with the required facilities.

Contents

Green As Grass

Do all waves rise from the Sea?
Do all rays fall from the Skies?
Do all things remain the same?
Through this broken journey of time?

Are all turns really needed?
Are all trees really seeded?
Did we appear out of nowhere?
Or did we form to wipe the trace?

Does one form to know a part?
Or is one born to pave a path?
Do all see the branches of time?
Or do all don't believe in lines?

Are we here, aware of all,
Or are we here to uncover a part?

Does only sentience feel green as grass?
Or does knowledge fail to last?

Should one step forward,
Into the dark?
Or should one strengthen,
The enlightened part?

We have all ascended to sense each change,
So should we ourselves Increase the range?
Should we go ahead, green as grass?
Shouldn't one fear the loss of the past?

We must all go and accept the change,
But won't we lose, with nothing to change?
Why knowing its wrong, we still stay?
Is fear wrong, are we just strange?

The Street Lamp

On a damp night,
Inside the womb of space,

Perching on a bench,
Life's warming trace,

Hidden from the shadows,
By the golden wings,

That kept floating,
On the cold shallows,

Soon the winds,
Joined the hurricane it could find,

It returned to abyss,
But the end intervened,

The spotlight calmed again,
But in the soothing silence,

A feeling of doubt surfaced,
Even the bird wash capable of violence,

Curled into sadness,
By the lamp of madness,

That flickered about,
Like the songs of rain,

Shielded by the thorns,
From the rose itself,

Your hands had been torn,
By the sword you held,

There was that street lamp,
You sat by,

Trusted the luster,
You blood made ember die,

Are we all really scared,
Of the air in the dark?

Would we all really perish,
With the end of the sparks?

The Sky Became A Lie

In ravelled worlds,

Where ends don't end,

In running winds,

Where Reality Bends,

An oasis came to sight,

But its strange gold,

Wasn't that bright,

a trap made for the blinds,

We strive to be broken,

And let go of life,

We hope to be frozen,

And still stay alive,

We wish to be Gods,

And bring back light,

But in the end,
Even the sky isn't high,

To tough situations, We all succumb,
Does it really matter what we become?
If to tough questions, we all fade,
Does it really matter if we are slayed?

We run far and get lost,
But we blindly chase the Sun,
We drown deep and can't sleep,
For a pearl, we all burn,

What dreams kill us,
While keeping us alive?
What fantasy pushes us,
To run away form the light?

What mind sees both,
A beginning and a demise?
What feelings take control,
Of your strength, your pride?

If mere dreams paint,
How as corpses shall we lie?
Can it really be,
That the ground begins to cry?

If a single memory shows,
How far we can fly,
Can it really be,
That the sky becomes a lie?

What ever we see,
Just remains a sight,
From us why do,
They seek light?

Masked

We wore masks,
To hide questions,
We tore souls,
To show satisfaction,

But deep within,
We drank deaduction,
As we shone brighter,
Burning our own sun,

Thought bit us,
We chased them down,
We were all consumed,
Wearing the drown,

Forcing the laughter,
We all went down hell,
Who knows through what ground,
All liars fell,

Masked and so were they,
What does it mean to live,
Keeping the door locked,
Or on open land you lay,

Why do people freeze,
When the masks they pull down,
Why do they need to please,
The high thunderground,

Corpses lay next to us,
Yet we see the soul fly,
Always finding roses,
Won't blossom life,

Why don't we see,
The danger's very eye,
Is it because we're humans
Or it it just a lie,

What we feel,
Might just not be right,

Do emotions weaken,

Or they help us strive,

Is expressing really a sin,

Or to keep society alive,

Is being masked,

Really helping the mind

Memory

Free from the poison,
Of the potion called life,
Freed from melancholy,
The one burnt alive
Freed from the mind,
The one with no life,

A disaster struck,
It stole the world's zeal,
It ended after the war,
The earth began to heal,
It faded into the force,
Of the ruthless memory,

Life ran chasing the future,
The past stood behind,
It was all forgotten,
For eternity it would last,

It faded into the force,
Of the ruthless memory,

A warrior won,
A battle of rights,
He was the lone victor,
With limitless might,
That soul faded into the force,
Of the ruthless memory,

As beings today shine,
Their tomorrow seems to be dying,
As their fading light flicker,
The truth becomes thicker,
They all fade into the force,
Of the ruthless memory,

Why is it so,
That memory has it all,
When will it end,
When will freedom reach us all?
When will it fade,
Into the divine tragedy?

The Window To Death

From blossom,
To wither,
It needs,
Nature's cover,

The smallest,
Mistakes,
It'll be,
At steak,

Why to live,
If you're,
Meant,
To die,

Why,
To feel,
The limited,
Sky,

Life,

Pointless,

A waste,

Of time,

I,

Wait for you,

For you,

To say 'Goodbye'

I,

Not for blood,

But pointless life,

Badly hurts,

Death,

Not to die,

Death,

Peace,

Life,

The chance,

To prove,

Yourself,

Life,

Short,

Don't spend it,

Dying.

Treasure Is Trash

Life, the harshest petal,
Softness hidden deep in metal,
The discrimination, never born to settle,
Always Unfair, the true battle,

The diving into shallows,
The searching for pearls,
The jewel not found,
The excitement suppressed,

Purposeless is your purpose,
To curiously wait until you die,
But that would only be yours,
Make other's lives smile,

The struggle's thorns,
You may strongly face,

The fiddled bonds,
May slowly fade,

Life not discrimination,
To strive, the last solution,
Importance just a lie,
Love will make you cry,

Treasure just becomes trash,
If living is just being lashed

Trail Of Life

A wheel tumbled down,
From the hills of peace,
It left a trail filled with life,

A gust swam down,
From the skies of harmony,
It cooled the flames of demise,

A ray was pulled down,
From a dawn of silence,
It's beauty had no price,

A gift was unravelled,
Revealing a sheet of gold,
But sadly, it wasn't tried,

Blindly, they all fell,
Into a trap cold,
Frozen, they couldn't fight,

Ragged and torn,
They still stood high,
In oblivion, they sought light,

Simmering in pain,
They tried to hide,
A frown out of sight,

They live dead,
Yet they know no fright,
The must stand up,
To be the world's guide

Traders

Seraphs of gold,
With a conscious bold,
Fighting the fates,
Of masses alone,

Down the thorny road,
Of the truth alive,
They bled out,
Covered their eyes,

They felt melancholy,
Course through minds,
To save their folks,
When the were dying,

Wounds were the traded,
The pain was sold,

To these mysterious traders,
To whose jobs we bowed,

Blown with the wind,
The sorrows of fall,
Scratching itself,
But wouldn't overhaul,

They drop down,
The orbs of life,
The blood was precious,
But so was the life,

Sorrow shown,
Over the plains of mind,
As they saw corpses,
Like they were the ones inside,

The doctors of peace,
They are the highest boon,
We should be grateful,
They keep us from doom

The Sight Of Silver

Why to look
and not eye?
Why to run
and not walk?

Seems to me
There's a lot to do
Why to act
and not speak.

Let your mind swim across the depths.

When you sight silver,
Pocket it in your heart, share it
Be a giver or know the sight still far

The silver you earn
might not be bright
But don't give up, yet
Search for a better sight.

The Fold

Light,
A chimera,
Striving alone,

Evil,
The act,
Killable,
The fact,

A chaos,
Twisted,
Destruction,
The loss,
Immortal affection,

The gleam,
A feel,
Rebuilt,
The stream,
Of zeal,

Peace,
A force,
Unknown,
The source,

The
Power,
And it's control,
The balance,
A fold...

The Flaw Of Existence

Terror sang, As being began,
Dark revamped, As the race they ran,

"What they've become, they can't stand,"
What they sense, they can't mend"

"Boasted by creation,
The past's reanimation",

They weren't creators, They couldn't define,
The truth behind meaning, It was fear all alive,

What we see, isn't always justice,
What we feel isn't always tender,

Existence wasn't survival,
Born to make us finer

Darkness

Oh can you see?
Oh can you witness?

A world so lost,
In the minds of thickness,

Oh can you feel,
Oh can you sense,

The dark crawl,
Into you head,

It soon will fester,
The pain will jaw,

Gone a rester,
None at last,

Oh can you touch,

Oh can you stroke,

The ghoul left,

In the past's smoke,

Is it really so,

That the dark is ready to knife,

Is it really so,

That the night is the end

Is it actually a truth,

That the blind can't defend

Clear

The lifeless sky that never existed,
The reasons that were left untold,
The light that was never lifted,
The air that was made to mold,

The empty depths of the disdain,
The feared aura of the loss,
The innocent cuddles of the pain,
The blackened terror's gloss,

The bleeding streams of the silver spikes,
The ephemeral feel of the sympathy,
The chilly breeze in the brightest of the night,
The nightmare of the terrific antipathy,

The clear sight of the unknown water,
The tearing height of the untold hesitation,
The fearful rights of the clutter,
The gate to the world of distortion,

The truth behind our eye's lies,

The reality that sunk into blood,

The lost effort in their tries,

It was all just hidden in the "Clear"

Blind But Still Alive

Withered people
In a quick sand
Heart pumping
but still morbid;

Melancholy dripping
into the pool of nothingness,
yet the blind is alive,
A deprivation,
that might start a flight,

The body might die,
But soul will survive,

Why a deprivation?

A never ending depression.
Why a life
Poisoning the mind.

Why a bird

caged but flies?

Why bullied,

for limits of better sights.

Able but un-able

Blind but still alive.

Spectacular Feast To Your Eyes

A spectacular feast to your eyes
To your mind a venom but
The sight refreshing, the touch wild

A pack of hundred pins that lies
On a beautiful rose that cut
A spectacular feast to your eyes

When far away, it looks nice
But coming near, it hurts
The sight refreshing, the touch wild

A spark that defeat the ridged ice
Isn't enough to escape the rut
A spectacular feast to your eyes

A tide captured wise

Yet pulls you to deep rut

The sight refreshing, the touch wild

Some things appear a prize

The rose, the moon, the snow harm

A spectacular feast to your eyes.

Teacher

Of none in the ascend,
Neither wither nor bloom,
Of emptiness in the void,
Neither joy nor gloom,

Of none in the afeared,
Of none to hide within,
From waters under no skies,
From where shades blended within,

Of none in the change,
Of none to restore,
Came a new start
To the end that came before,

But on lands so dry,
Where only sand roamed,
Of a promise never made,
The world couldn't get blown,

Upon a fear of crumble,
The world won't stumble
In disappointment,
Let all loss mumble,

This gust of wind,
The wings called teachers,
Of peace, a hint,
Fall's breachers

Down we looked,
And lied below, the lies,
Lifted from vortex,
A shame bestowed, by the eyes,

Ran up the flight,
Which shattered before the form,
It looked down to the sands,
To where it now belonged,

From the stairs to the wind,
The wings shall ascend,

From dust to the ground,
This was what teaching meant,

They tear away a feather,
To a newly formed life,
Only because of them,
We live and not survive

Chasing Horizons

Eternal, an illusion,
To escape the delusion,

Imagine what never was,
Forget the past,

The insanity kills you,
But never let it go,

Just see, what you can't behold,
Feel it, Feel it stroke,

Then see where you go,
Chase infinity, chase horizons,

You may end up,
But not what you have enlightened,

Chase beyond the world of dreams,

Chase the horizons,

The life saving streams

The Souls The Wind Holds

Wind blows, The force lows,

A stream, straight from ferment,

Maelstroms, skirmishes,

The chaos burnishes,

The seraph, shines,

And fades, away,

Darkness dies,

Healing the gay,

The demons, they slay,

The ways, they strike,

With misery, they sway,

Cogently, this is their way,

They all become, one,

When the beasts, play,

The weak they overcome,

Never do they delay,

With a power,

They glow,

But, They just,

Fade away,

The souls, the wind holds,

The roles, they play,

Weeding, as it blows,

Kindling the day...

Dreams

I locked up all doors,
And all gates to my eyes,
But I still could see it,
And my vision couldn't lie,
A barrage of light,
From a crevasse run loose,
I still was stuck,
Haunted by the ooze

I peeked out from gaps,
And all the peace in my mind,
From all little windows,
Broke in the light,
The ghost crept within,
Into the shadows of white,
And tore apart forces,
That held the burning night,

I looked up at the doors,

And to the heavens high,

But then it struck me,

A being with no eyes,

Known was no right,

Left me alone,

my dear might,

Where have you gone

I looked back to see,

Weather I gained flight,

I looked back to see,

Weather I feared heights,

Sorrow locked my brain,

But the keyholes weren't stained,

As I shed tears,

To a truth so bright,

I looked back to see,

If I felt free,

As I peeked through the hole,

That colored my face with glee,

I felt no wings,

Yet my eyes looked straight,

Through the yarn of blood,

Called our lives,

I feel something warm,

Caress my skin,

As it slowly tears,

Through the fear within,

I feel the pain,

In me it's dying,

Stealing the stains,

To myself I can't be lying

Cursed Corpses

Oh please just solve it,
Please just answer,
Why I live the way I live,

The mistake of existence,
The blunder of survival,
It haunts me as I strive,

I see myself being born,
While I am already,
Painfully dying,

I doubt the truth,
I doubt my life,
As I feel I'm bound to die,

A leaf that has fallen,
A rebel gone to heaven,
Now the roots to life,

As I fade away,
Petals shall blossom,
They shall be my afterlife,

We live on blood,
While letting it drip,
Down the path of life,

Perfection, a myth,
The progress, a punctures,
Pain hidden in gaining might,

A weak tower,
On which we fight,
It bares the weight of our rights,

Why O Why,
Does pain need,
To be the base of life,

We stand confused,
Because we have realised,
We died so we could survive,

Our tokens of victory,

Are our own corpses,

Buried alive,

We all just smile,

In a world that's broken,

We blindly strive, to not be taken,

We are breathing corpses,

Cursed by the force of loss,

Here we stand, just trying to surmise,

We are filled,

Brimming with lies,

All to hide the depressing cries,

The Earth's Song

In the moonlit black,
In skies ever so dark,

In the oblivious nothingness –
Hidden was a majestic spark.

In a trap called similarity,
That drove time to insanity,

In an illusion of deadly sincerity,
This realm seems to lose clarity,

The same after dying,
What's the point in this lying,

We all keep on cheating,
The differences, crying –

We hope of power
That bends tragedies,

We get the longed for flowers,
But along with thorny calamities.

It is the divine faith
That builds a path.

The loss fades,
Because it sold the start.

Forgotten but lifted,
A world that has been twisted,

The truth insisted,
But our lies resisted,

It seems to be,
We weren't really apart,

We were all just blood,
In a worthless heart,

The moon shone,
In the blinding dark -

It was just a stone,
The truth left a mark,

We all were pieces,
Of the earth's song,

Together a fantasy,
Broken along,

To taste the knowledge,
We all just die,

Never acknowledged,
But now we can't try.

Blood Of Gold

What's the curse in me ?
What was purged from me ?
What did they think I am ?

Just an insipid rock,
My lure, mock
Light had me knocked,

I look to be bold,
Why I think I am sold,
Naught is all I hold,

Bleed my eyes,
My sorrow it rides,
Callous tides,
Callous tides,

A monster they behold

To eternity sold

My blood, gold

The blood of gold

Drippings Never Heard

Rain,
But scarlet,
The pain,
A thorny part-let,

The spirits,
Call,
When in the void,
They fall,

The world,
Doesn't feel it,
The pain,
Nobody steals it,

Curse,
Not magic,
Jealousy,
And tragic

Down,
They face,
To the dark light,
They race

A candle,
Shines,
But their devil's
Shrine,

We give,
Our hand,
But they have,
Already fallen,

Their prisms,
Shone,
In an absence,
Unknown,
In an absence,
Unknown...

Drugs

Drugs drugs,
The biggest thugs,
They rob your soul,
They break your heart,
They are a poison,
that kills you fast.

Attractors,
Killing distractors,
They take away
your X-factor.

Brutal lyrics,
Corrupt phoenix,
A scented axe,
your mind it hacks,

So, say no to the pills
that fills you with guilt.
Say no to drugs,
to these mean thugs.

Say yes to life,
Open your eyes,
Open your eyes.

Fear, A Door

In places of mystery,
Where all terrors begin,

The closing gates of destiny,
The cries, they send,

In places where shadows lurk,
And wastelands of pain,

In regions of memories,
That left a stain,

Strange fears lurk,
Into minds creating brawls,

Apocalyptic times shine,
On courage, they all dine,

A barrier purging through the life,
The choice of darkness or light,

It fades away as you see it lie,
But instead of venturing,

You rot and die,
A piece of core,

Broken by the corruption,
Stuck inside an ore,

The disastrous eruption,
A burning world,

It will force cries,
A searing swirl,

It will help you hide,
A broken God will make you fight,

A burning sword will bring you might,
In searing pain only will you gain flight,

As you tear apart, you will seek light,

Fears are the doors,

To a world freed from gore,

Panic, A feeling,

The strength, revealing

Midas, Retreated

History alive,
A mystery insane,
Nature strives,
A lion with no mane,

Important but futile,
It costs all your smiles,
Can't behold its own power,
A dead flower,

A star with no light,
An eye that can't see,
A minaret with no height,
A being who can't feel,

A power but a curse,
A boon that became a bane,
The lion with no mane,
It was him but now its us,

We're the one to
Break nature's trust,

His possessions,
Were cursed,
He was sold,
To his own gold,

Its Midas,
Retreated,
What we touch,
Is polluted,

A king,
Lost his daughter,
But we will end,
Hotter,

His mistake,
Couldn't be undone,
But ours can,
Stop pollution,
Stop man

My Freedom

Melancholy trying,
People dying
for having a mind,

Everything, but nothing,
Those thrive,
Tho are begging.

The world chasing your sight,
You seek a companion in life,
A trader of unlimited heights,
Your final chance to survive.

A jewel
Your independent mind,
What a callous miracle,
Death at times.

Freedom to me,

A never ending freefall,

Humpty Dumpty on the wall,

Sitting, I relish it all.

Oil In Mind

A cook oiling the furnace,
In a rusty old kitchen,
And suddenly it lights.

The deluge that brightens the box
The disaster that rights the wrongs
The spark that splits the room,
The flame that paints the cave,
Hot

The painter slipped through the gaps
A bottle is too small to hold on ocean,
Can excitement be consumed in a celeberation?

Passion hunts for idols
In a world of aimless people
And soon a star is born
Passion spreads into others,
Discerning the spirit of talent
And rises from within the unexpected.

Rhythm Never Broken

A beat,
It's everyone's core,
A feat,
It's everyone's soul

An angel,
The merchant of magic,
Incredible,
She undoes tragic,

The light ,
Of whole crowd,
Their might makes
Millions proud

In their eyes ,
The future shines,
They taste words,
They create rhymes

Their words,
The door to success,
They are the busters of
All our stress,

Without them,
Who would tell,
What is heaven?
What is hell?

A rhythm,
Never broken,
A doorway
Gets open,

She lights's hearts,
She is a star,
She ignites compassion,
Could end all

The mother
And a child
The nature
Of life

The loop
If torn,
The cosmos
Will die

The rhythm,
If ever broken,
The feelings ,
Will get frozen

Scarlet Tree

Blood Blossoms, in the waters of trust,
It glows dark, with a disastrous lust,

The chains crumble down,
Unleashing the demons of frown,

Living Dead, Breathing lies,
Seeing tragedy, They built their own demise,

Melting reasons, Breaking life,
Consuming hatred, they all just die,

Survive and strive, In a realm of curse,
Hope, a lie, When suspicion emerged,

A cage of gold, Treasured debris,
A disastrous world, born of greed,

The clock tick, But times don't change,
We were all tricked, Into a blinding game

Simmer If...

An angry man,
About to shout,
Always ignored,
Will surely explode,

A conflict,
Warm,
Will split,
In swarms,

From vapid,
To horrendous,
The destruction,
Tremendous,

From ghastly,
To exciting,
The fire,
Can't keep hiding,

Insanity,

Kicks off,

But never,

Let it go,

Like life,

Nothing,

For ever,

But the simmer,

Doesn't,

Die,

Like dying,

Nothing,

Better,

But the storm,

That feels alright,

Never known,

When,

Will it,

Ignite,

Blindly,

Bright,

A clamour,

Calm,

A feel,

Beyond control,

Sealed,

A pressurised core,

Even one,

Wrong,

The death,

Strong,

The simmer,

Repeated,

The loop,

Completed.

"Spectacular"

A godly,
Thief,
Hardly,
Wrong,

Learned,
The ability,
To be,
Strong,

A lady,
Golden brown,
Running,
Its peaceful town,

Nectar,
And a sting,
The efforts,
Behind spring,

She stings,
To die,

Not making,
Us cry,

Workers,
And queens,
A kingdom,
Indeed,

A soft,
Miracle,
The lively,
Lyrical,

Her guild,
An Oracle,
She builds,
The jungle,

Bees,
The secret,
Behind the world's,
"Spectacular"

O' My Dear

Mist enveloped the poem,
Penned by the time,

Leaves came from stone,
The forces were alive,

O' my dear salvation,
You chirped on the branch,

Of the scarlet that shone,
Ever so bright,

Cried, the skies,
As crystals showered down,

Made a rainbow,
As your wings they torn,

O' my dear freedom,
Of sails so tender,

Yet still, all along,
They rebelled against thunder,

How could you have fallen,
To the rains divine,

Had you just forgotten,
There wasn't an end to time,

O' dear explorer,
To the heavens go trail,

But please remember,
You never failed,

Where you found light,
You stood strong,

O' my dear bird,
You never were wrong

Raided

Fear tore the kites,
Killed were the lights,
Crushed were the brights,
Horrors broke the sights.

Cursed was the night,
Purged were the rights,
Quelled were the tides,

Dawn could never arrive,
The brave burnt alive,
For luck they had to strive,
The survivors were naïve.

The days had fallen,
The gates never rose,
Destroyed was the realm,
Sadness and woes,

The zeal ,

A beautiful feel,

It was all dead,

The rain turned red

Nature faded,

The beauty was raided

Infinite In Finite

From alpha to zeta,

One hides strong,

From a penny,

To peseta,

One lives,

Long,

From candle to sculptures,

The wax isn't wrong,

The last drop they give,

With thirst they live,

The stairs they become,

In ravines deep,

A teacher,

Infinite in finite

The Reacher,

To goals near trinity...

The creatures,

Slaughtered with infinity,

They live to help,

But are made to die,

The one legend,

Now the one sighs,

The world doesn't see,

Being mentor being guide

The Egg

Dead,
Went high,
Shattered,
By the sky,

In darkness shone,
A light,
Lost my soul,
But had to try,

I held the sand,
It slipped off my hand,
I held the fire,
It burnt my desire,

I was left helpless,
Trying was my business,

To the force,
I had to surrender,
Just as a leaf,
I was left tender,

Soon I heard a crack,
And nothingness shone,
In the melancholy,
I saw entities unknown,

Their intelligence,
Had to be respected,
They saw things,
From another perspective,

They knew no fright,
Their thoughts couldn't be held,
For us they were light,
They always excelled,

The cosmic egg,
Will stay tight,
Till the whole universe,
Reunites

Rusting Skies, Golden Winds

From rusting skies and piles of dust,
From a broken mind, sharp gusts,
From distorted sight, death's lust,
Glows out a petal, bright,

From pale wind and fading faith,
From the whimful pity of world's grace,
From blood scattered in empty space
Blossoms a petal, bright,

In war grounds of scarlet mist,
In places of pain, that eden missed,
On leaves that couldn't be swept away,
Rebellion grew, ready to fight,

All beauty will die away,
Wind, a force, time has slayed,

In deep trenches of stillness,

Rebellion grows, wars for light,

Why only winds take away, lies?
Why only rewarded, by dawn's light?
Why, for what, does it thrive?
Fixing reality, losing life,

It flows by, and again, goes,
Remember, of it, all blossoms rose,
Thunders and Rains, the path it chose,
Power and will, on the corpse, it grows,

In skies filled with golden winds,
A promise to open, the mystery within,
Pleasure came from a lifetime of sins
The gusts keep smiling, with or without skin

The Fold In Time

A flicker in time,
A glitch in the clock,
The frozen flame a line,
The kaleidoscope, a block,

The fear froze,
The death rose,
A strong minute died,
A unit worth a night,

The memories were fickle,
The world became sicker,
Alteration ended up,
Just being a liquor,

The joys began to prick,
Feelings were tricked,
The fold in the time,
Sins started to rhyme,
Sins started to rhyme